VERSIONS OF NORTH

versions of north

G.P. Lainsbury

poems

CAITLIN PRESS

01 02 03 04 05 06 16 15 14 13 12 11

Caitlin Press Inc.
8100 Alderwood Road,
Halfmoon Bay, BC VON 1Y1
www.caitlin-press.com

Text design by Kathleen Fraser.
Cover design by Pamela Cambiazo.
Cover photo by Ahmed Mater.
Printed in Canada

Caitlin Press Inc. acknowledges financial support from the Government of Canada through the Canada Book Fund and the Canada Council for the Arts, and from the Province of British Columbia through the British Columbia Arts Council and the Book Publisher's Tax Credit.

Canada Council for the Arts
Conseil des Arts du Canada
BRITISH COLUMBIA ARTS COUNCIL
An agency of the Province of British Columbia

Library and Archives Canada Cataloguing in Publication

Lainsbury, G. P., 1962-
Versions of north : poems / G.P. Lainsbury.

Poems.
ISBN 978-1-894759-62-5

I. Title.

PS8623.A39555V47 2011 C811'.6 C2011-904940-6

For Ezra & Tanya and the girls.
"If *love* be not in the *house* there is nothing."

"What is involved in the composition of a long poem … is five to ten years."

—John Berryman

"You have to go into a serial poem not knowing what the hell you're doing."

—Jack Spicer

Contents

Scenario 1: The Energetic City

"To be dumb and have a job, that's happiness."

—Gottfried Benn

I. Paramount Regime of the Normal

"By closing its doors from Oct. 3 to Oct. 30 the Fort St. John Public Library hopes to make up a $26,000 shortfall in its budget."
—*Alaska Highway News*, Sept. 14, 1999

it is an almost impossible space here
we inhabit our Authenticity
the design-specification of conscious mind

forever indulging the chronic atomization of consciousness
following leisurely patterns of dosing and contemplation
our desire for industrial & financial growth continues

unabated further evidence of the strength
the persistence
of metaphysical need

when language goes on holiday the question is begged:
"Why (or how), in an era of total information,
is everyone and everything deceiving us?"

we sit and watch
the mainstreaming of the financial
its dangerous masculinity

making it impossible even to go into
the damp overhung valley
w/out being poisoned

we are guilty of plagiarism
& affective reconciliation
self-regulated citizens
caught in eccentric representational orbits

so we need to indicate our sources
(two miles beneath the moon's surface)

become demons of the bloodiest kind
this desire for transformation
bespeaking our intolerance for the unspeakable

(the fleeting and incidental by-product of the workings of selfish DNA)

the giant beetle with fever-shaken thorax
workman as appendage of machine:
do they know that to remain sensitive
is a utopian stance?

god bless those who hustle
pursuing the bewitchment of intelligence by language
conceptual assemblers
seeking to secure
the full vertical density of reality

yes we were a good and loving invention
our cynical enlightened false consciousness
the happiest thing left to us

& yes we noted a general increase in loathsomeness
as those boom and bust cycles
flash from gold to silver
grow purple and massive from a distance
disintegrate downhill
in avalanches of sand

thank goodness people's right brains have been eaten
by roboticized steel rats

II. The Delirium of Uselessness

"If we closed the hockey arena, then there'd be … riots in the street."
—*Alaska Highway News*, Sept. 15, 1999

let's cut off his head respectfully
this saint for thugs and gangsters

it is probably common knowledge that this project
was to bring untold wealth and prosperity to the region
words hazy & inflated through centuries of exaggerated feeling
based primarily on the oil & gas industry: promoting
a climate of drunkenness, brutality & degradation

he sits up nights brooding everything that is the case
the idiocy of rural life
animals as persons
words that make coffins break loose and walk off

search for a smiling christ
happy teaching w/out pupils
able to enjoy shopping malls

after all jesus doesn't just belong to the Xtians anymore

so it is okay
to have as latent ambition

making the world's last unpleasant experience
a precisely dateable event

says he to whom no one is listening
of whereof one cannot speak

it is not the function of a presumption to presume
the generally improbable:

thereof one must be silent

for we are unhappy pigs
our loftiest arts nothing but
mood-congruent perversions

even if we have amazed by our deep sufferings the thing itself
this perfect vehicle for dramatizing
the subtle permutations of an era
preoccupied with private liberation

art weighs down the thinker's heart
& creates in populations a longing forever
to bite and devour

socialization through schooling: *a priori* stupefaction

if only the rebellious subjects of America
would endorse the discursive trope of the familial
walk through the enchanted gate
offer flesh to pacify him

then maybe the world of objects at rest might allow
a transnational free market in psychotropics
a table adorned for a feast without food
an ethos of permanent revolution

such playful estrangement the result of utopian wonderdrugs
which reinforce and enrich our most cherished ideals
creating a hyperdopaminergic sense of things to be done

the sky is still a black void
intermixing private, political and universal instrumentation
to penetrate events:

it has a lot of information

Scenario 2: Consumerland

"To write a poem after Auschwitz is barbaric."

—Theodore Adorno

I. Industrial Hub

"*mens rea*—the presence of a guilty mind"

he reconsiders his mastery of the strange & bizarre:

"the definition of dead has changed, I tell you!
they threw the body off the bridge
into the Peace River ..."

so through summer days
we sit drinking coffee on the wooden steps of our cottages
consider a project of cultural fitness

the imaging of Indians
as self-perpetuating industry

he thinks he is made of dust
is a jar of bumblebees
shaken & opened
in the face of a young playmate

no mere reaction to the cult of domesticity
a childhood *grand mal* seizure

but now I aspire leave behind rainy sidewalks of the mind

ideology of the gaze
refracting pleasure and authority
great vortices of energy and power

"we'll let the gooks be the Indians"

& perhaps take the monumental view

she has no wish to be food nor
a pastoral image of self-reliance

she sings about gardens:

"once I styled myself
the double obscurity of Saskatchewan
those shifting rhetorics of self
the most selfish act
I could commit"

the creek gushes
over green boulders into
pools no human ever uses

Japan gets richer and unhappier

exigence calls genre into action
he clutches a handful of brushes
as a rainbow bursts through
a woodsy landscape behind

"Better yet—let's write an official poem of protest!"

II. Frontier of Empire & Wilderness Playground

"the righteous anger of the court pierces the corporate veil"

the have-nots are given spending vouchers
as compensation for living lives beneath refinery smokestacks
their children get drunk and kill people
while claiming to have been
all the while standing outside themselves
watching it unfold

but the golden arches are tumescent
& cast a semiotic glow
over the strenuous life

the Lazy Künstler and the Well-Travelled Monkey ask
if one's ambition is vulgar in its magnitude
(consider the poignant hollow husk of Mr Wasp)
perhaps one should give oneself over to
lying dissolute and melancholy on the ground?

or is your ingenuous profession of laziness
only a conscious holding back
a reflexive suspicion of power?

(have you been taking things for granted?)

it is her job after all
to make him feel better
him being he who says least
puerile rebellion reduced
to unthinking aesthetic essence

but most of the things he thinks about
are of no importance to her

genre as social action
corporate semiosis
an episode of the Lone Ranger involving a black widow
hygienic governance & social morbidity
the apogee of the asset bubble
the fluttering of an anxious middle

(also she thinks he is stupid)

always

the sea somewhere booms
a stream rushes loudly

Scenario 3: Dreams of Exile

"Writing sad, crepuscular poems … while the world was in flames did not seem to us either strange or shameful."

—Primo Levi

I. Cemetery Criticism of the Partly Fogged-In Past

"We spent the declining years of the American Empire like so many others, pursuing our private interests in the geographic space assigned us by the economy."
—Sid Squalidozzi, "Why I Am So Miserable" (*Ecce BiPoHoMo*)

(to be able, at least, to romanticize
one's situation, even if hopelessly
infected with cynicism, a sign
of mental health, however tenuous)

that first Xmas driving back from Calgary
through a critique of emerging meaninglessness
an ethnology of death transcendent bleakness of *taiga*
Swan Hills Waste Disposal Facility
a station of my Gulag Archipelago

"so where is this world they are advertising?" she asked

our visions are distorted by the gravity of
a strong representational orbit
not to mention an entropic longing
for extinction

what is left? when armed with only
shrunken experiences & subservient languages
of banality & despair but to attempt
to stitch together a work consisting
entirely of quotations

to mark one's place
in the useless dispersion that is the universe

[Originally established by Alexander Mackenzie as a trading post in 1794, Fort St John is the oldest European-established settlement in present-day British Columbia.]

II. Zones of Contact: the Homeless Mind

"... men of my age, and especially the least likely ones—have been noted as liable to strange outbreaks, belated uncanny clutches at the unusual, the ideal."

—Strether Martin in Henry James's *The Ambassadors*

in fact, I'm really trying to explain that I don't think I'm
obscure

raising the hidden onto the table   trying to find
a way to justify beating up on others
in the name of fixing the system

all that passivity and spectating of misery
just part of the job

"there are" he thinks   "too few souls for all humanity"
as he works the everyday consciousness of the vanguard
to provide market economies w/homogenously educated employees
taking medication for depression for 20 yrs allowed him to be

productive

-are you radioactive, pal?
-has you the night sweats & the day sweats, pal?
-do you float on a silver stream of impunity?

or like the workers of all countries   forced through
the applicant funnel   so as to avoid the perils of
the Cathedral of Erotic Misery
& become citizens & servants of
language   free
of Aristotelian historicism   able to project
a world as moral-optical illusion
to entice those younger more "warped" traditional
girls
forgotten into dream & awakened only
by music
evoking brainsick fantasies of morbid
cobweb-spinners & a romantic
Egotistical Sublime that
might
be the most real being if

we weren't so decrepit sardonic catatonic w/
fewer genes than a block of wood
we wldn't need to fuck
to prove we're alive
or articulate links across
discourses &
fields

our Disgust & Overdetermination at odds w/our desire
for an infinitely small vocabulary
& not so latent epistemophilia
conjunction of "empowerment" & institutionally buttressed
amateurism
a single projectile charged
w/all the power of the Universe

predicated on & productive of the disavowal of economic concerns
that is at the heart of bourgeois existence

Geo Stanley's "mainstream": a river of blood & garbage
moving through a landscape
expanding round circles
like
the opening of giant parasols
indicating acceptance of *de facto* complicity & the necessity of
sacrilege
imposed upon the titanically striving individual
sublime Aryan active sin as highest
Promethean virtue

positivity as
compliance, spiritualized

& of course
Death is a German expert
the most unpleasant character in all of fiction:
jealous & proud of it petty unjust unforgiving a malevolent bully
capricious & megalomaniacal his
mythical juvenile dream sagaciously & arbitrarily transformed into
historic-pragmatical *juvenile history*

thus the professor is ideal personification of inertia w/out
inertness

by nature more articulate than dependable relating
outtakes from a continual debate inside his
head
his defences obsessions
& addictions
techniques of qualification digression metonymy
a tendency to right hemisphere activity
associated
w/negative mood & anxiety

frivolous & eccentric as an old man
when the masses threw themselves at his feet
he reversed his own tendency

she became suspicious because her horse was acting strange
& getting infections
<“Parm me, lady” “Orright”>

do you have the discipline
to talk out of the part of yourself that can love?
myself can hardly
stand to touch my person to someone else’s
it’s this damn aesthetic disposition the disinterested consumption of all manner
of cultural objects
for their own sake
that leads to fewer mating
opportunities
not to mention the psychic burden
wearing oneself ragged w/brain
always on high alert
while for others
simply not fucking apparently willing young girls is clearly
a challenge
the epic side of truth— *muthos*
fucker
hey—it’s the only *polis* you got! either this

or dowsing for dummies w/Peter
Culley!

III. Ghost-Town Elegies

"& I'll tell you—it's no big thing anyway, to be a person, with a Kind of life, yet that's what people are interested in. . . ."

—George Stanley, *Vancouver*, Part 8

the master plan—to bring all into related registers of
Cosmic American Fellaheen music

eschewing dat vision obscured by dominant
modes of being a populist w/an elitist's vocabulary
& a slacker's persona   sporting

a special variety of openness
"terrified tenderness"

to satisfy the expensive girl of his anguished dreams
he is compelled to put on a performance that is originary
in its ambitions & embarrassing in its excesses

rippling in the quick of his skin   heedless & real
he verbed fer 40 yrs
shot & buckt

standing on a pedestal of ice
a sublime &
slightly sinister
conductor
of bad karma   one smashed open his head w/
baseball bat whilst others   went at him w/barbecue forks &
barber scissors
one might say vocabulary did this
but nobody said anything
while those ruthless assassins of indigenous   *Quechua* origin
ambush their solitary victims
drain fat as god-offerings
getting wrecked   & messy
forever in the winning & losing of weird underworld regattas

so when thinking you are losing your head
consider the long pome as feasible
& culturally necessary!
or at least as sort of barricade 'gainst their
massive data structures

not to mention that 90 kg chimpanzee named Travis
who's threatening to rip off your hands, nose, lips & eyelids
citing a systemic sadism
inscribed in ethos
of American
exceptionalism
& tremendous advances in prognostication by "consciousness industry"
cybernetic folding as enactment of open-form poetics
a global machine for springing surprises
blending infrastructures of subarctic adaptation w/ that of an historic archaic
postmodern treasury of the familiar
whilst enduring freaky mystical night drives
on roads shared w/amphetamined gas daddies

reimagining the behaviour of women
in terms of his & hers relativeness "here-
ness"

moose leap across highway in drug-fuelled frenzy
oblivious to the ramblings of that god-*dämmerung*
Baptist radio operator
saved! by a
slow mind &
a tendency to drift
in an act of bravura vanity
this technophiliac, tough-guy & toady
composes complex pivot-tables
out of insider rhetorics
of anecdote & conversation
bloody emissions cluttered w/snakes & jewels & bile &
arsenic
putting aside everything outside
exploitation
momentarily to consider
the hindering of marriage by eros
not a problem of limited resources
but deployment & temperamental destiny
the heteronormativity of gladiatorial yob-gods
to be distinguished from non-functional neurotic anticipatory
pain of The District Psychologist's Ex-Common-Law Husband
& his bands of brothers tunnelling through mountains of shit
such monotheistic gravedigger mimicry
an extreme example of Ditch Vision

both carpenter & condemned clearly see
scaffold
while the scopophiliacs disappear abruptly
muttering that "it is in the administration of rhetoric that the thinky death consists"
& we kant get rid of God until we lose Grammar

meanwhile, somewhere
bipolar girls meets narcissistic boy
convicted rapist lives in home w/ten corpses
fucking & talking & talking & fucking
half-empty bits & pieces
inhabiting grey pebble-dashed houses
referred to in the
literature
as "neo-vernacular hutches"
they dream of the English Exit touching the cat w/out a glove
know it will come w/pain in mystery
systems on the edge of chaos
in states of self-organized criticality
is as much as I can stand
of all this "good life" dogma
those state whores dress up as
Sophia saying what they don't
know
about scapulimancy
& individuation as origin & cause of all

suffering
their performative scholarships just
make me wanna
ruin
everything

Intertext: Lyric Fragments

Out on Bail

freakboy, we miss ye
& those epic battles:

the innocent Vivian Girls vs. the evil Glandelinians

so convincing
we all believed for a moment
we were tragic

however
i don't think the judge is buying

"the lived necessity of critique" as alibi

not w/those fingerprints
that dust on the police car hood

The Psychopathology of (Northern) College Life

"You run on *ahead*?—Do you do so as a herdsman? Or as an exception? A third possibility would be as a deserter... *First* question of conscience."
—Friedrich Nietzsche, *Twilight of the Idols*

a place where all
are neither fish
nor fowl

the secretary
just a bit too smart
to be satisfied
managing
a mid-size office

the teacher
who doesn't really
like kids

or who kids
don't like

or who can't
keep his mouth shut
at meetings
work well w/others

all those MEds
w/academic pretensions

the MA w/connections
&/or charisma

various permutations of
the academic
not interested enough
in her subject
to continue work
beyond the dissertation

the frustrated professors
w/out proper lecture theatre

too much libido
for priesthood or wife
sublimating desire
endless preparation
jogging

the English instructor who
stutters & blushes whilst reading
the dirty bits of the books
he assigns

the historian
who writes potboiler novels
replete w/racial stereotypes

the wildlife biologist
who chases bears
from the staff parking lot

the chemist
w/record of research
obsessed w/*lebensraum*

the physicist
who just can't understand
how his students can be
so stupid

the Muslim mathematician
starving through Ramadan

&, of course, the smug
superior bastard
w/a few poems
in magazines
nobody reads

Coronary Dis-ease

(for Barry McKinnon)

faced once again
w/the paralyzing complexity of the discursive world
one might just decide
silence
the only possible
response
[better than another
feasibility study?]

not to mention
the wide range of punishments
available
for the persecution of
transgressors!

or the extensive
availability of reward
for those
who can eat shit
& smile
implement
ministry policies
collect
names of those
who claim damage
nod & smile (again) & bow

Oil Wives

"In revenge and in love woman is more barbarous than man."
—Friedrich Nietzsche, *Beyond Good and Evil* (139)

as recently as five years ago
this group of community-minded women
united by a certain social status

gathered at the Mackenzie Inn
every 2nd Thursday at noon
devoting themselves to gossip
& good works

there are still some of these quasi-genteel types around
self-made but mellowed by age, having assumed
posts on the board at Lakepoint

the younger wives just aren't the same:
marrying young & indiscriminately, they know
almost nothing but that husband will be in camp
much of the year

no worries but for income, for the purchase
of the incredibly gaudy ring she proudly displays
to the salesman as she prices ever newer & larger
more expensive pickup trucks, to hire
personal trainers, rent time in tanning booths
all in preparation: her side of the deal

assuming the object-position in a stripper-fantasy
when he returns late from the Condill every night
for two weeks after spring breakup

if she is young & particularly beautiful
& he dare even suggest a limit
to the extension of her credit

her eyes will begin to dart around the room
assess the situation, look
for one more pliant, with an even bigger
income, who can fill her w/even more
good stuff

Unnatürlich Künstler Ich

unreal life—
(of course we knew
death had undone
so many)
one of *those* days
prone to ecstatic relapse
(drugs
kicking in)

seeking balance
this new psychopharmacological regime:

edges smoothed
skin thickened
humour coarsened

now others need not treat so delicately
for we are euphoric

& then
the wet black bough
kick
in eye

car parked
front of Lutheran home

woman
rocks
back &
forth
in seat
grips
steering wheel
face
distorted
animal mask of pain

est-ce-que une autre rêve?
that glance sideways
distorted

by need
to see

something
like this?

what monster
this narcissism
that informs
our figuring
violence
abstraction

the wheels of the artist-mechanism
turning

Argument

hey baby   it's all coming back to me
& I'm writing it down in   lyric fragments

& by the way—do you & your friends
know who you belong to?

enough of this silt breccia nonsense   [ooo la la!
such a stone cold fox   "let's have some interspecies incest"
watch varved clay draining fossiliferous
Devonian limy shale   podzolic soils form in
summit craters

as love is a function of death
i'm happy to be the target
of the bite that is
your smile

allowing me to be
a little less
not so suspended
in a discourse of permafrost patterns
i surveil my modern arctic
munching on the brains of small children

until again i ask: can you make it work inside?
amongst these closely spaced mounds   this network of
troughs
might we dissolve ourselves into
universal background radiation?

go ahead, baby
drive that remote control bomb
under my chassis
snuggle it right up
there

let it rip

Scenario 4: The Problem of Everyone Else

"… we know our neighbor exists because he's outside …"
—Italo Calvino, "Blood, Sea" (*t zero*)

I. Town and Country

"It goes without saying that there can be no democracy, or even an on-going project of a democratic society, without autonomous individuals capable of critically and imaginatively participating in this project."
—David Wallace, "In Search of a Democratic Aesthetic"

now   all our weak   sinful   rebellious subjects
let us gather to talk of
doing the work: civ/n
not out of nostalgia for a supra-temporal community
but a need "to overcome one's estrangement from which one is
most familiar"

to correct the national body
fixed/
hetero-

let us stop   pulling stone knuckles from the earth
our meditation upon southern money
like rumors of rain
the geography of apocalypse: roadblocks & barricades
the trembling poplar w/silver leaf
torment of metal / scream of saws
darkness upon the plain

geniuses: a dime / dozen elsewhere   here an inflationary regime

our inhabitants include: rig hands in doghouses
whole villages from Cape Breton
one who doesn't know what a suntan is
the alcoholic driver & the catskinner
recent parolées from federal institutions
economic migrants from dying prairie towns
bars full of sad promiscuous & angry souls

they're often really fat & their clothes too tight

so whatever happened to distributing people intelligently?
must we resign ourselves once & for all
to that helpless   destined feeling?
accept survival as its own reward
secrete an establishment around ourself

assume a sidestreet vegetative excrescence
alongside our sceptical neighbours
their faces stubbled w/frost
long johns on clothesline slanted slab-hard in wind
ragged edges of crop pleating into riverbank

gathering the dispossessed & displaced
arm muscles unencumbered & armpit hair fully ventilated
taking every opportunity to antagonize
the boar half-starving from winter's sleep

how many of us seek a country where nobody else lives?

manifeste cannibale dada
a state of intoxication sanctions all irregularities
catastrophic emissions cover
the velvet rind of branches
w/an exuberant verdure

among indoors people   facing frosted windows
populations assembled for no compelling reason
the harshness of pioneer life: immense cold   poverty   no electricity
no romance

living in Bad Faith
people live quietly underneath flight patterns
playing w/rifle as if it's a woman

fucking one's subject

while overhead satellites report to companies   locate facilities
plumes of toxic material: matter out of place
death as short-term effect of exposure

is there *no place* free from (this) presence?

living together must allow for repetition
tolerance of those who come to work
planning only to stay a year or two
just long enough to put a stake together
pad a résumé

all symptom of plethora
here we may skip stages in our *bildung*
get whatever is needed
watch wild berries swell in the pagan sun
herons feed in watery meadows

& who could forget our summer companions gnats & mosquitoes?

yes here is only an interval even if
enlivened w/vast herds of elk & buffalo
numerous examples of the Abandoned Farmhouse
genre

all available for the cost of distraction psychological & otherwise
the old jail across the river
where industrial culture went to dream
address among
brooding pines its moodiness & other spiritual
infections
contagion always a risk its capacity for punitive retaliation
written in accord w/a canon of the self-forbidding
internalized as commodification of social agency:
to be finished would indeed be a relief

but there is to be no distraction from this incessant chatter
political rumblings from the south
so we gather accessories to show how hard we work
& how we are *always* working

our willingness to endure /
this dreadful freedom

the barren reaches

this is what happens as the silver fangs of the mighty axe
destroy this magnificent theatre of nature
the strippers clean up & streets go unpaved
the vigilance & severity of the husband
his affirmation of self & desire
to complete the truncated precursor is humiliating & tedious

whereas a wife's normal contribution
the equation of virtue & masochism
an unmanipulated sorrow
clashes w/his proneness to side w/beauty

the result a certain lack of care:
ugliness filth squalor relationships
subject to sudden & / or violent ends the job offer
from afar the call home

in the spring giant frost heaves & potholes erupt

the eye's revenge:
those blue depths moon forsaken
thick hair of poplar & spruce braided across sky
save where the birches grew
deeper more complex formations

dead things were all about me and the year was dead

II. L’escalade non anesthésée

invoking realms of the unreal
that trance of wonder   that doth run through nature everywhere
even as we
cross the meatloaf line:
observe now the decorative function of trees & animals
motors discharging in response to anxiety
graffiti tags on dirty brick walls &
buff old urban *ayahuasqueros*
mixing systems   producing fresh desires

from the north   death   a fog comes down
to put forward the unpresentable in presentation
flaunting raw data   the many deaths
we had delivered

"this was once a city"
proclaimeth George Stanley to those assembled in the parking lot
"this plastic rose" now inscribed in our species-being
a moment in the history of capital
a dumping ground for scum
a vanguard machine   dragging humanity after it
hungry ghosts
everywhere: chaosophy & the inevitability of annoyance & risk
a focus for all problems of poetics

those annoying others   who also inhabit these places
take   for instance   contestant #2
a remedial semiotics student
he fits the profile!

suckers appear on his head   he studies
the illusion of an enduring understanding &
the American bourgeoisie interlude
how   despite such an extensive array of competence-building measures
some people get headaches

Jamie Reed evokes "the labour aristocracy" (big-headroom people
tend to be predators, ingesting & expelling identifications)
a grievous stream of analysis terminable & interminable
a range of vision beyond that of ordinary people

(& we always being found innocent for "ridiculous
reasons")
drinking w/poets & thinking ab't nothing much of the time
this be the position of the late-modern self, *vis-à-vis*
the brown meat & its insatiable insistence on chasing primal
ecstasy

while the common-sense discourses of the soul would indicate
such time as is better spent planning & producing
customized learning-objects for One Big College

Scenario 5: & Them w/an Ontological Stake in the Past

"... contemporaneity—both in nature and in human life—is revealed as an essential multitemporality: as remnants or relics of various stages and formations of the past and as rudiments of stages in the more or less distant future."

—Mikhail Bakhtin, "The *Bildungsroman* and Its Significance in the History of Realism"

I. Nowhere, Our Mutual & Eternal Origin

"The world it is a winding-down ..."
—Sid Squalidozzi, *Sophisms & Soporifics*

& where do we begin but nowhere
the vacancy that marks the spot we are all
rushing from   place where universe
itself was born in an event barely understood
by the arcane & elegant mathematics
of our physicists?

maybe w/lucid indifference   everything

an immense world spun into being by offbeat equations

["boy   gotta get on
that Messianic timetable" thinks the listless dreamer
immersed in his flaccid life

a slightly decrepit figure
sitting in an old barber's chair
perched on the edge
of the Mojave
desert
sings old George Jones songs
searches the skies
points into the deep past
brings attention

to a location on the ice-free corridor proposed as migration route
from Alaska to central North America in late Wisconsin time

now a wilderness where converge plains, boreal forest & Cordilleran economies
occupied by indigenous peoples
& savaged by industrial
intrusion
here it is we situate
the Old Timers &
the Natives

so, the overriding question:
can we avert   chronic
impending disaster?

an early glaciation moves in from the east or north
1st damning the ancestral Peace

2nd ice sheet moves in from northeast flowing
in a broad sweeping curve
as if deflected by the Rocky Mountains
or ice tongues
issuing from them

[& us, caught stupid w/the delirium of parenthood in that
Cordilleran ice sheet reaching to w/in 15 miles of FSJ late in Pleistocene
leaving behind a fan-shaped pattern of drumlins & glacial grooves

waking to consciousness of youth after dreaming middle age
becoming ice free very early in post-climactic recession

inheritors of the truly original inhabitants of the Americas
split by a knife-
sharp cliff
predicated upon laws of composition & coincidence
a twice-repeated succession of gravel overlain
by sand silt & clay

walking above a crimson sea of fire
throwing medicine at each other a style of discourse
working through of a politics via
ecological imperatives

senses stirred up / vibrating
this intellectual taste for the unhealthy
focuses upon high-centred polygons
of unprecedented height

coarse pink silica-cemented quartz sandstone from the
Athabaska Formation]

but he
will never love again, ache longer perhaps a pair of adults
will complain ab't the three men who beat them w/baseball bats after leaving
the party

all of these moments
in the life of a northern Indian community
suggest failure of the moral treatment
of mental illness

*   *   *   *   *

it is said he chose to live like that
face haggard, sinister ravished & malign
witness to countless violent event-scenes
above stream-eroded Cretaceous bedrock

a reaction to the predominance of the hollow form
a base aspiration for worldly goods
overcomes the better angels of ourselves

but lacking in belief we
adjust
our Metaphysical Positioning System
factor in
that cosmic lightning &
thunder smell
& a dark clay described as
"black, unctuous & impalpable"

try to shut out the set of noises invading our
dream
vulgar revisions & the promiscuous
intermingling of commodity
associate personal experience w/mythic archetype
assert idleness as precondition of artistic production

so savouring the failure of his life
she shoved a tray of icecubes up his ass
to prolong his agony

keeping the subject conscious to design
a prospectus for an enterprise not yet off the ground taking
into account knowledge tectonics: content (ed/ly) drifting
dissolute impressed / through reminiscence

always-already its own transgression this ultimate
freedom: to live w/out anxiety
to burn forever rushing
hither & yon
under-medicated & liable to
the tribunal of the Little Hordes

* * * * *

what to do but make
a problem of existence eschew
the Now of Recognizability
return in the Real what is refused
symbolically

[they 1st appear in Berkshire censuses in the early 19th century
listed as agricultural labourers scholars, whose only passion
is smoking too much]

pay good money to attend
an amusement park of rhythmical gadgets
ride the trolley down onto alluvial fans
built by short intermittent streams cutting through
silt & clay of adjacent platform

this country which makes a direct impression of primeval lawlessness
& moral nihilism is judged perfect for inhabitation by those seeking
a letter of recommendation to the Association of Registered
Technicians of the Sacred & possessed of a pathological state of moral
scrupulousness

preparing to transform the human race enacting
transit from Imaginary to Symbolic Order
creating conditions to make such action possible
the post-Nation-State logic of Capital trails
stumps, dams & lodges as massive bodies of information
exuding
tedium

meanwhile
the stylization of existence takes home the beauty queen
pursued by fear that one day he will be
crushed by
family stories perfected in the hellish Forge of Domestick Recension

continues to associate   idleness & study w/
                                        the deep blue depth of things

a weakening of integration w/social order   reflects back
    the strident shallowness of life   suggests
    the emptiness of the dream, that all might one day
    live in palaces   leaving only

abusive language to be directed at people w/power

II. Nowhere, Everybody Knows This Is

"Ur-historical experiences of the collective unconscious engender, through interpenetration with what is new, the utopian as it manifests itself in traces through a thousand configurations of life."

—Walter Benjamin, *The Arcades Project*

"La la la, la la la la ...."

—Neil Young

three physiographic units recognizable in the Fort St John area:
- rolling uplands
- trenches occupied by streams
- intervening platform characterized by gentle slopes
  & deep deposits of unconsolidated sediments

here we try to affirm our own essence   while
anticipating the resistances of a   refined & fastidious reader
who lives outside the main paranoid power circuits

[he's extremely smart & sensitive & soulful & therefore
in constant & total pain]

the empty principle of universality   shows
no sign of erosional unconformity between till & base of late glacial lacustrine deposits
to justify shifting pathos toward   salvation of the oppressed

so we remain w/in   the historical prison   of primordial
human nature
subject to instinctual energies   dark forces in the blood
try to keep out of the way   dodge the
dark mattering of scorpion-shaped
shadows
opt for the projection of causation onto others
the progressive enticement of the weak by the strong
drugs & prostitution follow the money

small-scale band-level societies   interspersed
w/the paraphernalia of oil & gas exploration sprouting up everywhere
disorderly splinters of the once-great machine
[but still of top priority in the schedule of utilities—much higher than
merely "knowing something": to think & plan through dream]

the essential Satanism of commerce pawing the
ground in place its remarkable preoccupation w/literal truth
into whose jaws thousands of bulky young oilfield workers
& drowsy clerks must hurl themselves every
morning

a few think it a great idea
to live a tragically excessive life
die a tragic hero become immortal

modernity signs off suicide
the ultimate interference w/latent if potential
will-to-work

alluvial gravels & overlying
floodplain silts
mantle the terraces & floors of major stream
valleys
chert pebbles w/no known source

* * * * *

before cable television
when it was still okay to think ab't
Indian people as the proper & inevitable subjects
of objective & imperial social science

the lake was a formidable barrier during the summer months though
islands & promontories on the far shore wld be visible to encourage
man on his journey [following retreat of ice sheet the
development:
a series of ice-dammed lakes]

before the individual shamanism fundamental to N American hunting
cultures was displaced by the wildness & chaos of uninhibited spree
drinking cowboy clothes rodeos homespun & populist
conservatism

before smalltalk narcissism condemned us to perish in self-sublation:
the use of language to silence restrain coerce

flashing what he has w/the back of his ear
the thing-in-itself behind the appearance of work
[cliff-head dunes above actively wasting shale slopes]
finds fault w/the imperfect expression
of a grand & sweeping emotion like
Calvinist grace known only
through outward sign

panoptically aware & appalled by
the unwillingness to follow wounded animals we send for
giant person-eating animals of mythic times
to pursue those hunters w/that special sense of display
[antlers of prize kill mounted on truck]
& render that crude device
through which they experience reality w/
questions that stick like fish hooks
so that the yoke of reason might be placed round their necks
allowing them to also enjoy the nervous irritability
of the individual devoted to solitude & thus enter
straightaway into the heart of harmony
a state of motionlessness & detachment

parabolic dunes appear locally

there is a genetic relationship between gravels & valleys
inter- or preglacial gravels record a river flowing
from the Rocky Mountains after draining of Lake Peace streams
establish themselves in interglacial trenches &
a late-mature stream-cut topography emerges: thus!
the lower Kiskatinaw flowing through a series of
spectacularly incised meanders
landslide deposits: deformed & brecciated Pleistocene silt & clay
marked by hummocky topography

dynamics of stability & change in a northern hunting culture
stations at the long end of the spectrum w/
extremely low population density, even for
hunter-
gatherers

meanwhile back at the ranch the professors & their eyes of lichen
impossible to impress metaphysicians
of sport inform a theory of pessimism work to limit infinity
piece together what history has broken into bits

[a 29-year-old woman tied up & beaten repeatedly w/hammer by three men]
by reducing the possibility of socially counter-productive self-advancement
these all-purpose declarations of alienation indicate
the origins of history in gossip
[a better life in a good cabin w/no neighbours]

*   *   *   *   *

i walked ab't   trying to protect my head w/my arms
one of the innumerable waves in that mighty flood
when hundreds packed the arena to watch Saturday night hockey

the horror   the boredom & the glory
all those years tweaking the input   asking
"where do i end / you begin?"

the innermost core of bourgeois coziness
this most unnerving & celestial of girls   releases
the sweet pollen which interferes w/logic   unleashing
the fierce & massive intoxication of the stampede

our attempts to reduce the denominator of the happiness fraction
predicated upon a *focus imaginarus*   from which the perfected
system might be discovered

we felt ourselves
growing poor in threshold
experiences

[one notable gravel deposit is remarkably clean apart from rare mud lenses]

confusing our decline w/the death of humanity
style bites into & penetrates the reader
following the Swedish model   guaranteeing relations
of individuals to the tasks required of them   even those
not able to walk long or fast enough to keep out of the cold
while aspiring to a total absence
of formal hierarchical structure
constellating: to bring dialectics to a standstill
a moment   in Indian time

[outlaw gangs compete for the Energetic City's growing drug market]

two hypotheses both of which present problems dreams
through which hunters & animals come into contact w/each other
immigrants travelling steerage from Marseilles on hellship

oh, to take leave of the past gaily to trace
the thin gold of imagination through a rocky mass of metrical gab
its ascendancy measuring the recession of the dream

hateful little clusters of houses crowded together by planners
to achieve economies of administration & service
local accumulations of detritus from a wasting ice sheet
indications of fornication lie flaccid in the moiling mud

the incorporation of nihilism into hegemony presents
an incurable imperfection in the very essence of the present
the need for refuge we find in childhood neurosis

combining calculation & reverie
Muskrat's experience at the moment
when image becomes
substance
guiding subjectivity to accept prescribed social roles

mute & weary southerly trending glacial grooves
heaven to one side of but at same level as
the point where the trails to all animals meet

the old North becomes the new West

III. An Infernal History

"I would like very much, though it cost me dearly, to discover a truth capable of shocking the whole human race. I would state it plainly to everyone's face."

—Joseph de Maistre, *Les Soirées de Saint-Pétersbourg*

the dreamy epoch of bad taste
a well-defined erosional interval following the older glaciation
an interglacial age indicated by pebbles of red granite & gneiss
chert & white quartzite erratics of supposed Rocky Mountain origin

remainders of the excluded   a Scottish country lane   an
ambitious boy driving a milk cart
reads from the book stashed under his seat
Jude dreaming   a world   a legacy
things in the context of
their redemption

standing terrified outside the walls of Jerusalem
thousand-year buds pop open all around me

[thicker accumulations of sediment on floor of lakes at mouths of tributary valleys leads to establishment of main stream in topographic low along distal wall of interglacial trench]

let us then evoke the cowboy image: proud, aggressive, competitive,
vain, maudlin, controlled & violent   this is all thought worthy
by proponents of the energy frontier   dreaming their permanent boom
the six-wheeled epic hero   the hardest of hard hats
the blissful ecstasy that wells up from the innermost depths of man

industrial passion:
an adequately intelligent variant of moral idiocy

[massive till & rich clay characterized by scattered pebbles & boulders]

in the wings struts   the hero of sensitivity
feeling like he wants to kill people   all the time
this excessive, non-functional cruelty   demands
an outlet   distinguishing idleness & work-preparation
job descriptions of an absurd future   distracting children   for
a living   a poetics for depression

maybe this is why we is all so unhappy   being where we is
    even our summer gathering place: Where Happiness Dwells   now
        consigned to corridor   status   no place in itself
      but mere   conduit to elsewhere

[gravel littoral & deltaic deposits overlain by aeolian beds or swamp deposits]

the nothing that is   future collapsing into present
    a jump in careerism & practicality   calculus of immediate options
        the World Secretariat for Precision & Soul
      aspires to a flabby stupor of mutual reassurance
    an affair of obscurants & expense-account industrialists
    a serpentage of aspirants fostering   life w/out benevolence
                destroying w/out malice

proudly born & raised   flesh & blood local heroes gut it out
                    in the corners   Thanatos
      reasserts himself w/a vengeance: love of debauchery

the analogy of intoxication holds fast the unbending of the wild curve
moving in a direction determined by sense of weather & "rightness"

    a conveniently sliding divide   stories always beginning
& ending
    adaptation over millennia to resource potential   post-Pleistocene
      boreal forest environment   thoughtworld of people
          knowing taste of every kind of meat
                    warmth of fur against skin

back to him whom the very dogs shunned   his Principles of Superposition &
    Original Continuity   allodoxy & complacency in spleen

        artifacts for which they had no artifice   planning so muted
        as to seem non-existent   stimulus to drink & dream a swarm
        of imps   restless   expanding & remunerative activity
        far from where its dreamers live   those genial scoundrels
        emancipating experience from event w/impotent cynical
            reflection
        [now that smells like a theory!]

*   *   *   *   *

this stony clay a "lacustro-till" a sedimentary facies
intermediate between till & lacustrine beds deposited
in standing water ponds & swamps floored by a yellow-orange
calcareous silt & loamy sand

[a seeming infinity of land makes everything seem possible]

to be in all this a moral lever to prise open our own
condition: ruthless, savage & rigorous
conquering God & the old life in a last struggle to attain
the grand style in Art even w/
our constitutions delicate owing to want of attention to
personal comforts & unrestrained use of ardent spirits
a resolute indifference to wealth accumulation yet
this newest remains the same song: eternity of hell

[then comes the turn; the speaker's identification becomes literal ha!]

drunk on virility obsessed w/rank
winged indecision moving in terror from bar to bar
the lector w/no method but ethos configuring
the Now & Then: dialectics at a standstill
loneliness at centre a central & disintegrating force

[laterally directed pressures accompanying growth of ice wedges in intermound areas]

the external surface of unconscious events & extensive overlap
of activities are perhaps better lived w/out meaning

[: but how can a man like me be expected to live & work under such conditions?
: why, cast all thou hast into the fire, of course!]

people must be regimented because
they never do the right thing of their own accord
must be fitted to a primordial landscape of
consumption induced to a chronic consciousness of crisis
that odd state of soul when the void becomes eloquent

concealing our labours
bringing us all back home to the time before the new Safeway
before satellite dishes disrupted suburban rooflines
to when Dunne Za: real people whose events take place
only after being experienced in dreams their
adaptive success dependent on skill & knowledge of individuals

[he was stoned out of his brain   but knew a good idea when he heard it]

those slowly building temptations   to turn
one's back   on life

[gypsum crystals develop in place by reaction of calcium- & oxygen-rich ground waters
w/detrital iron sulphides]

authenticity reeking of mysticism & the police
the despair of the quick study: how much we can sleep
how little we can sleep   a stance of aggressive
aphasia estrangement coupled w/the uncanny   rootless
fetishizing of roots   hatred of home   American chemical
misadventure   an inexorable ferocity which even death cannot
relax
a menacing, hazardous massif   a man threatening
several people w/a baseball bat   sharp black falling
triangles   a complex pattern of connections between trails of people
animals & primary celestial objects
ending in a theory of boredom

Scenario 6: (coyote::moose::deer::dog)

I. End of the Postwar Communicative Pact

"They are burning the woods, the brushlands, the
grassy fields razed;   their
profitable suburbs spread."
—Robert Duncan, "The Fire"

because of shrinking forest cover
monkeys have increasingly moved into cities
beginning
a sequence of alienations   that make performing
proper subject-object relations
a game of mutual
parasitism

so you might ask
what is in front of my mind?
visions of royalty plums
being tossed   into the anus of science
capital levering
access
to gov't funds
conceptual garbage dumps where dangerous excesses of
imagination   are shunted
for disposal
now let us visiteth
the reality principle
an awakening that
happens while awake
full
of primitive German terror
& projectile irony   we abject ourselves
before its narration
of the everyday
its explication of the
obvious
maps authorial consciousness
over time   whilst simultaneously calculating
intermittent antipathy towards familiars
as well as the great value which vice possesses
for constellations of
daily life   not to mention consequent
necessity of the painful struggle   to educate
our natural dispositions

so that we might address
the infinitely demanding
call for justice
& the paradox of declining female happiness

obviously our long history
of over-promising & under-delivering
needs to be revised in the interest of a more passionate syntax (perhaps
something to do w/the remediation of commas)
or at least we
must move negotiating a symbolic price
to be paid for all our
unearned solutions
mobilize both method & its conscious application to serve
refutation

if only
all those others might slack a little we might enjoy
the intersubjective embrace of common understandings
master
the feedback signal between existence & possibility
instead of building our separate underground bunkers to work away the time
until evil lord Xenu returns
[of course it is easier to forget oneself in some functions than in others]

* * * * *

do we have it in us
to not join that terrible
frightful company
more interested in glory than grammar
dust off those ol' engineering studies
do new environmental werk massive
stakeholder & 1st nations consultation
utilize our special mix of crankiness, brilliance & cruelty
against the logic
of those
inclined by chemistry & reinforcement whose
early maladaptive schema
outnumber Averroës' calalogue of Anti-Mnemonics
& make most difficult the installation of ethical & normative values

no matter how
daunting the prospect
we must continue our northern transient relationships

fortify our white blood cells
against this assembly of grasseous elements
where visiting
herbivores snuffle & belch
go-betweens in the realm of matter
their skillful depiction of the superficial
is useful like Egyptian art
when monkeys are wreaking havoc

those revolutionary simpletons   their jerks of thought & vision
determination that life can be made yet
miserabler   a pure system of spasms   operating always above
the fluid dynamics of a unique institutional setting
the going rate for maintaining sanity
under increasingly insane circumstances

whereas once
the application of deconstructive method was thought to generate liberatory results
now affective priming disposes us to the execution of unconscious inclinations

ergo: the Happiness Project
our vanity of vanities

a formation of flying girls dressed like religious novices
in James St Vaults   accepting distraction as prime contingency of
capitalist living
cultivating eccentricities until they become full-blown disorders
anarchic agents absolved of responsibility for keeping thoughts moving
by a robust association w/depressive symptomology
those affectless bastards in charge
hold off formal approval until so far
down the line
it only makes sense to complete

all this time
sirens ring through the city as the drunks slam into each other
some girls simper pathetically in the presence of dour slouches
others wait for emotionally stunted boyfriends to grow up

or
a god of rescue who saves girls from
their situations   off & on
(nostalgia-ridden abscesses created by the constant motion of language

*   *   *   *   *

how best
to describe our experiences in beaverland?

becoming like
unto that
by which one is intoxicated
in such a way as to form or extend a rhizome of generalized reciprocity
a strait cut to heaven
a time when all might say
my life   my job   my home
& still feel clean
but eventually all mailboxes fill up
& life is perceived to exist
only to the extent that it allows
parasitical consciousness to feed
upon it
predictors of fear of the unknown come
to dominate this wretched hive of scum & villainy
its violent shame
out-of-control monkey troupes
substituting Abstraction for affect
a reel
Satansbraten
of indentarian confusion
a body w/out organs
bad brain of   WCW in hell
manifest as residue
site C wuz all he cld talk ab't
a detestable & miserable man but marvellous minor poet
to be in a room w/him drives people crazy
& always the neighbour across the hall notices
a strong smell of body odour
every spring breakup
his lectures on the refusal of ambition
& music as uncopyrighted continuum
from which he freely plunders
resonate   in the air soughing w/the bawdy innuendo of eternity

II. There Is No God & Humans Are Essentially Evil

amongst all this

kung-fewshun

some claritas wld be nice

let's ask ol' Maggot Brain

aka Cowboy Mouth

whassup? still lost midlife in a dark wood
blazing w/hostility & feelings of defeated gigantism?

[all the while the local constabulary continue to have sex
in their marked police cars, on duty & in uniform]

slowly becoming aware of deficiencies in mindfulness
& autobiographical memory
its mad dance of self-enhancing productivity
that whole Heideggerian marmalade
how you stand in relation to the many realms
oscillating between suspicion of total futility & desire for total dominion
being particularly sensitive to cultural factors in the structuralization of
perception

dreamers
listen to animals dance & sing
block out the noise of "so many lucky men
restless in the midst of abundance"
always running
interpersonal deficits
occurring accidentally in a dehierarchized sequence of daily events
trauma of the symbolic order aggravates what's already in their heads
a psychic neuralgia
wholly unknown to normal life
where apparently it's still a novelty
for men to have sex w/an orangutan

[at least the cops are monitoring radios for duty-related calls
during their various sexual encounters]

how to join
the adequacy of what is told
to a mania for deepening collusion w/non-being

living off Mesozoic investments
history overflows ontology
in a tsunami of prosperity
our money so clean
its imageless affective presence
transcends that which passes for natural in me
both work & hatred derived from erasure of particularity
signs of infection & disease
theory emerging effortlessly from
ethnographic language
the long slide into happiness
unregulated behaviour, depression, alcoholism, aggressiveness,
interpersonal insensitivity
taking what you need & pissing on
the rest
increase dosage & dictate a necessary world
of sentient beings
context for our understanding relations w/the spirit that doth pierce
enveloping gloom

* * * * *

"so there we were, high on Yagé,
"lying around in a telepathic state"
fully aware
of the maleness we participated in
preoccupied anxious & depressed
proud pioneers bringing benefits of clean, safe nuclear power
practising an arid ferocious scholasticism
testing the limits of a denatured humanity
seeking almost continually to please
the girl just kept on getting
pregnant
by that bespectacled fellow w/his metallic procurer's voice
seeking the pathways that connect all sentient beings in the war of all against
all
her mouth comes to you
like the manifest rejoicing in quantities
a continuous
self-vibrating region
of intensities
trying to find the one in whom you are
a positive & active
anguish

tied forever to desire
[a dead Iron-Balance for weighing Pains & Pleasures]

liable

to grow in anything:
observez les people of the dream!
falling through the Happiness Gap
their wheel of desire
punishment for the adequacy of what is
thot closest to the visions things have of themselves
instant conductors seize passing matter & lead it harmlessly through me
growing rigidly attentive to glimpses of bared
athletic girl-flesh
our hero pulls a rat from 'is ass
amidst much
phenomenological parsing of reality

pale   limitless blue & green recessions
laced w/strands of scud

mark the solipsistic dead-end of the romantic lyric
beside which an orangutan from a prostitute village in Borneo
wuz found
chained to a wall   lying on a mattress
[if a man walked near her she wld turn herself around & present herself
start gyrating]
of course we're all desperate characters
& multiple biological relationships do breed complexity

but surely   the animals
at least
must remain   holy

always he w/most to hide
leading calls to openness
self-serving individual biases inevitably undermining cooperative activity
women always in a hurry
jobs whose uneventfulness wld be unbearable if not for the abundance of 1st class
opium
even the most reasonable people make errors when they think
under fire

*   *   *   *   *

w/deconstruction as inheritance
our obsession w/crabs, homosexuals, tree roots, the slime
of being a $3.5 billion / 900 megawatt question, poignant
evokes negative affect, tension, lack
of responsiveness, overt & covert hostility
amongst those divorce-prone individuals
writing in the guts of the world of work
stories realized in the theatre of their telling
decline of plants & birds
freedom manifest in highfalutin entertainment
& Boethian reframing tactics

of avoidance & atomism
vicarious trauma & compassion fatigue
merging depressive illness w/self
eyes roll upwards in skull

she strips herself
of every purpose
to catch a voice
from the unsaid
regulative object of interpellation
big box drugstore w/
guard-tower motif at Spy Hill
a more optional, less permanent institution
lying under generic substrate
these lovely guilty people take refuge in scale & Shabu
[a local variety of methamphetamine]
to master the glimpse
it helps to have a kind of indifference on one's side
to participate in an abomination larger than oneself

squeezing lines

into pictures

composing

turds

breaking
Planks
over the head of *Hodos*
chameleontos
one is what one knows
in this theatre of appearances
our perceived self-efficacy domains
allow us to get the boss off to one side & give him a pump-action earful

experience the ecstasy of Gestalt
those negative aspects more salient than
mot der gism & bomb kultur

totalizing downward incompatibilities of modern life
delirium, hallucination & wracking nausea
taking an unprovoked swing at desublimation
both city &

country wives
tired of this Uranian atmosphere
taking crazy things seriously
modelling her isolation

love

made angry knows
loneliness like a spouse

III. Zones of Contact

living in the desert of the
Real
the purely egological initiative of the political subject or
what the young puritans wld call a waste of fucking time

at the risky moment of waking
scattered elements of world come together
herd-like w/in receptacle of consciousness
infused w/holy spirit & stupidity enabling
confidence
we locate two twin-unit ACR-1000 Advanced CANDU Reactors
on a site 30 km west of Peace River
[$6.2 billion / 2200 megawatts]
our fetish as dream congealed
from the repertoire of boyish gestures
including contempt for virtuous deeds
universal reservations towards one's own way of life
an endless parade of lethal desirable things
uniquely marked & fretted
by clinically relevant perfectionism leading to dysphoria & despair
[scent of her armpits holier than prayer]
an economy driven by smugness
our versions confounding our visions
status anxiety & positional wealth
attributing misfortune to malevolent thoughts & actions of other people
one becomes what one thinks
blood spatter against wall the officer dragged her from room to room
his character an adaptation to domestic emotional economy
in a Neoplatonist cave of nymphs
the true & appointed setting of genius
contrasting harshly w/the fate reserved for beautiful women
beatings & banishment
["this will sure teach me a lesson"]
the slum of innermost being
abstraction as style of anxiety-driven processing
a faulty inferential process attributes negative events to global causes
young moose by roadside
head bobbing
nostrils steam w/bloody discharge
in the modern city the live man
feels or perceives this sort of thing
as the savage perceives

in the forest
oil fields inducing earthquakes
we become the "new energy colony" for our wealthy neighbours
allow the land to be busted open by the imperial suicide economy
women try to protect their children by not calling
out during non-consensual sex
hypervirility constantly leaping
back & forth
cavalry regiments riding over her body

* * * * *

we tell our authors
to make sure they have income from other sources
to write so good nobody understands
that language through which light passes
to make products of the social brain
a source of private
enrichment
forget Poetics as a form of Life
remember
it's lank, not wank
& contradiction is close to the untrembling heart of thought
where depression correlates w/multiple marital transition
& early stages of remarriage
subComediante Marcos
conjures utopian feminista versions of perfect partnership
out of fear of major extinction

it all points to
something else
problems in deep cognitive structure
a pub-based apprenticeship
followed by senile onset of affect

[punk legend backed over by Safeway truck in parking lot]

to be relegated to repository for learning objects
totemic thought set in shamanic-cosmic structure
kultur-hero / transformer
overcoming giant person-eating Greek abstraction

["we too are interested in becoming wealthy"]

that we may make our life worth dying

[the couple engaged in aggressive & even dangerous "lovemaking"]

we seek revolution around every corner
embrace
full catastrophe living
greed, hatred, delusion
pharmacological optimism
& other errors in thinking
the outside that ceaselessly invades our thought
the self in its behavioural environment
scratching haphazardly on Indian graves
its filthy messages
just to make itself aware
it is thinking
if only we cld stop loving
the children
the burden of our humane effluent might eliminate shithouse gothic
as sincerest work of the world as paranoid art
Cantos as contaminated site
family not holding up well
huddled around radio
a mode of inhabitation in which tradition is transformed
by that most terrible drug we take in solitude
aversion to open air
expedient mendacity
traumatic banal hostility

* * * * *

so, finally
to summarize:
why fucking bother?
sure it wld be nice if folks down south cld generate their own power
& we know many people wld like to werk less
though always
we know ethically impeccable noble consciousness will pass
imperceptibly into servile base consciousness
flatterers & sycophants enjoy
swimming in shit
inattentive parents & notoriously unfaithful husbands

will continue their hyperinstrumental naming
reduce to minimal number of elements
make more negative, coercive & conflictual networks of
give & take
excluding that general individual described as peculiar
by correlation of intelligence w/depression & neurosis
allowing no creation of necessary artifacts from local material
no stepping out of the game of social manipulation
no divinatory practice
only tangible embodiments of volitional beings
& restriction of youth under ethical apprenticeship
we remain
islands of pain in a sea of misery

thoughtless & impulsive, & perhaps loyal, too, but above all else
cowardly

Note on Text

Versions of North is the result of over a decade's work of compilation and composition. I sometimes call it *Visions of North*; other times *Versions*, depending on whether I am feeling more like Jack Kerouac or Mick Jones.

In an early statement of intent I described *Versions of North* as a long, "serial" poem that attempts to situate the North in terms of avant-garde poetics, philosophy, sociology, economics, etc. It is an attempt on the part of one human being to make sense of the forces, large and small, that have brought him to a particular place, and that have shaped the place where he finds himself. William Carlos Williams's *Paterson*, "a long poem [written] upon the resemblance between the mind of modern man and a city" ("Statement," May 31, 1951), is an important point of reference. The poem is both more and less than an "Idea" of North (with all respect to Mr Gould); it is, in the limited sense that is always "my" sense, the embodiment of an uncertain North, weak and highly constrained by context.

Looking back through my journals, I see the impulse to engage with the local manifest itself in the longish poem "Ghost-Town Elegies," begun in September of 1997, about two years after I had moved to Fort St John, as I prepared myself for impending fatherhood. Another key event in the development of a shift in my poetic practice from the short lyric to the long poem was my meeting Barry McKinnon in the fall of 1994; I had recently moved from Vancouver to Terrace, and Barry's reading at a UNBC literary conference made a significant impression on me; his influence on my practice as poet and on this particular project are profound.

The project began as a formal exercise in technique, the utilization of postwar cut-up technology to circumscribe the linearity of conventional poetic logic. Over the years I introduced a drafting process which included image-collage as the background to the emerging poem—the process of composition has been captured on video, which can be viewed on YouTube under "glainsbu." One day I will get around to mounting the complete set of image-intensive drafts of the various scenarios that make up *Versions* on the web.

Versions is appropriate given that each mounting of the work is constrained by the technology of presentation. The work is first done on eleven-by-seventeen-inch sheets, and "reduced" for chapbook publication to a seven-by-eight-and-a-half-inch page. Trade book publication has necessitated further work to fit the constraints of the page size made available to me by Caitlin Press. Thus my most observant readers will note that line breaks and spacing vary considerably in the various publications of the work over time, reflecting my interest in an improvisatory gestalt.

Finally, it must be said that *Versions of North* is a work of massive integration, with many "sources" and/or appropriations. An almost certainly incomplete list of such might include: Clement Greenberg, "The Avant-Garde and Kitsch"; Margaret Atwood, "Singing to Genghis Khan"; Elizabeth Smart, *By Grand Central Station I Sat Down and Wept*; Leona Gom, *Land of the Peace*; Patrick Lane, "Bunkhouse North"; Ludwig Wittgenstein, *Tractatus Logico-Philosophicus* and *Philosophical Investigations*; Karl Marx, *Manifesto of the Communist Party*; Friedrich Nietzsche, *Human, All too Human*; David Lenson, *On Drugs*; David Pearce, "*Brave New World*? A Defence of Paradise Engineering"; Brian Fawcett, "What is Wrong with Alice Munro?"; Peter Sloterdijk, *A Critique of Cynical Reason*; Zbigniew Herbert, *Report from the Besieged City*; Walter Benjamin, *Illuminations* and *The Arcades Project*; Denis Johnson, *Jesus' Son* and *The Throne of the Third Heaven of the Nations Millennium General Assembly*; Italo Calvino, "Crystals"; William Gibson, *All Tomorrow's Parties*; René Thom, *Modèles Mathématiques*; Andre Gidé, *The Immoralist*; John Berryman, *The Dream Songs*; Jacques Derrida, *Acts of Literature*; Thomas Mann, "Death in Venice"; HG Wells, "Zoological Retrogression"; Herbert Marcuse, *Eros and Civilization*; Theodore Adorno, *Minima Moralia*; Slavoj Žižek, "Multiculturalism, or, the Cultural Logic of Multinational Capitalism"; Pierre Bourdieu, *Homo Academicus*; Alexis de Tocqueville, *Democracy in America*; JD Salinger, "Raise High the Roof Beam, Carpenters"; William Burroughs, *The Yage Letters*; William H Gass, *The Tunnel*; Thomas Pynchon, *Mason & Dixon*; Martin Amis on Roman Polanski; Henry Miller, "Letter to Anaïs Nin" (December 10, 1932); Robert Musil, *Man Without Qualities*; Robin Ridington, *Trail to Heaven: Knowledge and Narrative in a Northern Native Community*; CS Giscombe, *Prairie Style*; Ted Greenwald, "Whiff"; Libbie Rifkin, "Making It / New: Institutionalizing Postwar Avant-Gardes"; Samuel Beckett, *Murphy*; Gilles Deleuze and Félix Guattari, *A Thousand Plateaus* ...

Previous versions of the Scenarios that constitute the poem have appeared in: *Post North III: The Truth, House Organ, stonestone, Norther, The Capilano Review, Queen Street Quarterly* and *It's Still Winter*.